CONNOR McDAVID

HOCKEY SUPERSTAR

BY KAREN PRICE

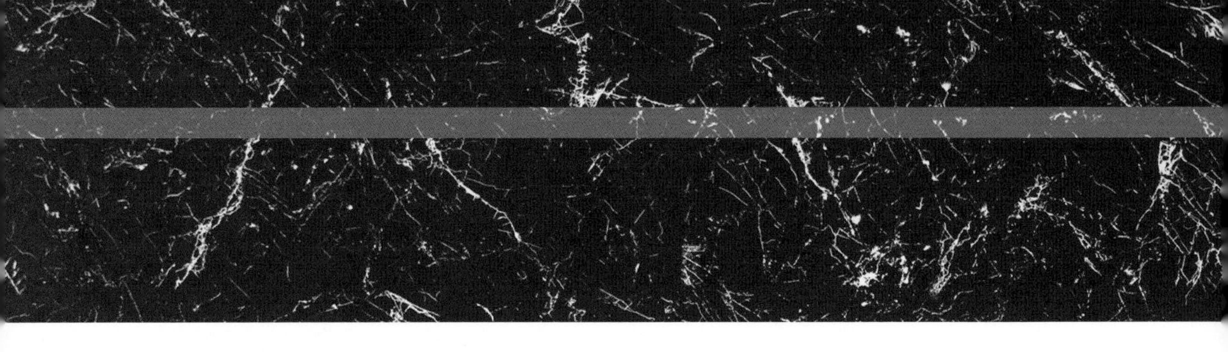

First Edition
First Printing, 2019

Book design by Jake Nordby
Cover design by Jake Nordby
Photographs ©: Curtis Comeau/Icon Sportswire/AP Images, cover, 1, 22, 30, back cover; Andy Devlin/NHLI/National Hockey League/Getty Images, 4; Jason Franson/The Canadian Press/AP Images, 7, 8–9, 20, 27; marinat197/Shutterstock Images, 9 (rink); Jack Hanrahan/ Erie Times-News/AP Images, 10–11; John Crouch/Icon Sportswire, 12, 15; Andrew Dieb/Icon Sportswire, 16; Bob Frid/Icon Sportswire, 19; Amber Bracken/The Canadian Press/AP Images, 25; Red Line Editorial, 29

Press Box Books, an imprint of Press Room Editions.

Library of Congress Control Number: 2019936731

ISBN
978-1-63494-103-7 (library bound)
978-1-63494-112-9 (paperback)
978-1-63494-121-1 (epub)
978-1-63494-130-3 (hosted ebook)

Distributed by North Star Editions, Inc.
2297 Waters Drive
Mendota Heights, MN 55120
www.northstareditions.com

Printed in the United States of America

About the Author

Karen Price grew up outside Philadelphia, graduated from the University of Colorado, and has called Pittsburgh home since 2002. She has been writing about sports for more than 20 years.

TABLE OF CONTENTS

CANADIAN
OILERS
CCM
97
62
C

1 FOUR GOALS

Connor McDavid lurked near the net, waiting for an opportunity. He and the Edmonton Oilers were facing the Tampa Bay Lightning in February 2018. Early in the first period, an Oilers teammate snapped the puck toward the crease. McDavid was ready for it. He thrust his stick forward and deflected the puck into the net.

The Edmonton crowd erupted in cheers as the horn blasted. McDavid's goal gave the Oilers a 1–0 lead over one

McDavid makes his way toward the net during a 2018 game against the Tampa Bay Lightning.

of the best teams in the National Hockey League (NHL). And McDavid was just getting started.

MORE THAN JUST A NUMBER

McDavid wears No. 97 because he was born in 1997. Growing up outside Toronto, he was always the youngest player in the leagues he played in. But he was also one of the best. His number sent a message to his opponents. It reminded them that they were getting beaten by a younger player.

In the second period, McDavid streaked toward the goal line. At first it looked as if he would bring the puck behind the net. But when he was next to the goalie, he fired a shot. The puck passed behind the goalie's back and went into the far corner of the net.

In the third period, McDavid stole the puck at his own blue line. Then he exploded down the ice on a breakaway. The goalie knew what was coming, but he couldn't stop the shot.

The Edmonton crowd goes nuts after McDavid scores his third goal of the night.

Fans threw their hats onto the ice to celebrate McDavid's hat trick.

Later in the third, McDavid attempted a pass. The puck bounced off an opponent's skate and went into the net. It wasn't pretty, but it was the fourth goal of McDavid's amazing night. He had shown why many hockey fans consider him the sport's brightest star.

McDAVID'S SECOND GOAL

McDavid was nearly parallel to the goal line when he scored his second goal of the night. He shot the puck behind the goalie's back and into the far corner of the net.

97
CCM
CCM

2 TEENAGE STAR

Connor McDavid started playing hockey when he was just four years old. When he couldn't be on the ice, he shot pucks in his garage. Sometimes he even practiced outside in the rain. He loved watching hockey on TV, especially when Pittsburgh Penguins star Sidney Crosby was playing.

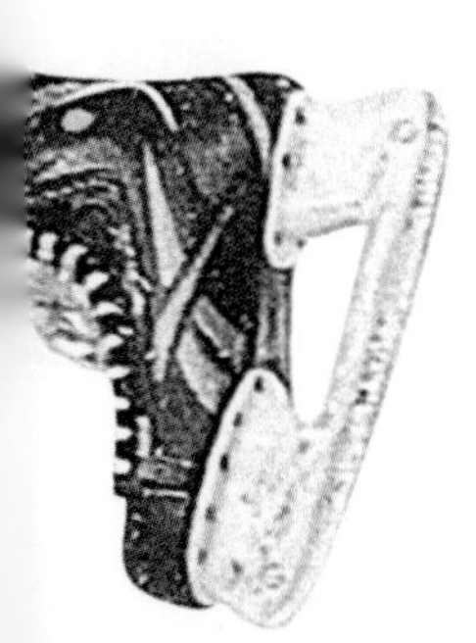

When Connor was 15 years old, his parents decided he was ready to play junior hockey. There was only one

A 15-year-old Connor McDavid competes in a junior hockey game with the Erie Otters.

Connor attempts to skate past a Niagara IceDogs defender during a game in 2014.

problem. The rules said he couldn't play until he was 16.

To get around those rules, Connor applied for exceptional player status. That meant he needed to prove he was good enough to enter the junior hockey draft early. He also had to show that he was mature enough to be away from home and keep his grades up.

It worked. Connor became the third player ever to get that special status. Everyone else in the draft was a year older. Even so, the Erie Otters picked Connor No. 1 overall. And right away, he proved that he belonged.

At age 16, Connor was named the league's rookie of the year. By his second year with the Otters, people were saying he could be as good as Wayne Gretzky. That was high praise indeed. Hockey fans generally agree that Gretzky was the greatest player who ever lived.

In McDavid's last season with the Otters, he was named Canadian Hockey League Player of the Year. He also won awards for academics and sportsmanship. And even though the

Otters lost in the final round of the playoffs, McDavid was named the playoff MVP.

In June 2015, the NHL Entry Draft finally arrived. The Edmonton Oilers held the first pick. There wasn't much drama, though. Everyone knew who they were going to choose. McDavid sat in the audience and looked around nervously. Oilers president Peter Chiarelli made the announcement. The Oilers had selected McDavid. His NHL career was about to begin.

O CANADA!

Connor McDavid became a star player for Team Canada when he was a teenager. In 2013, he helped Canada win gold in the under-18 championship. With eight goals and six assists, he was named the tournament MVP. Two years later, McDavid was playing for the under-20 team. He scored a goal in the championship game to help Canada win another gold medal.

Connor attempts a shot during a 2015 game with Team Canada.

17
BAUER

POULIOT
67

3 IN THE SPOTLIGHT

Connor McDavid had always been a star player. But now he was in the NHL. The players were faster, stronger, and older. Everyone was excited to see McDavid play, and expectations were high—especially with Oilers fans. They hoped he would help bring the Stanley Cup back to Edmonton for the first time since 1990.

Just three games into the season, McDavid thrilled fans with his first NHL goal. In a game against the Dallas Stars,

McDavid celebrates his first NHL goal.

he was skating along the boards. He saw a teammate get the puck near the blue line. So McDavid peeled away toward the net. As his teammate shot, McDavid poked his stick out just before the shot whizzed by. The puck connected and tipped past the goalie. McDavid let out a whoop and skated past the bench to slap hands with his teammates.

McDavid's first month in the National Hockey League was an impressive one. He scored his first game-winning goal. He had his first multi-point game. And he won his first award as rookie of the month.

Unfortunately, the next month didn't go as well. In a game against the Philadelphia Flyers, McDavid got tangled with two players while driving toward the net. He crashed hard into the boards. McDavid stood up slowly and skated

McDavid scrambles for the puck during a 2015 game against the Vancouver Canucks.

to the bench holding his shoulder. He left the game with a broken collarbone. Even worse, he missed the next three months.

McDavid returned in February for a game against the Columbus Blue Jackets. He was in

McDavid prepares to shoot the puck past Columbus Blue Jackets goalie Joonas Korpisalo.

front of the home crowd in Edmonton. During the second period, he received a pass at the red line. With his feet churning underneath him, McDavid skated toward two defenders. They were closing in, trying to cut him off before he got too close to the net. A third defender chased close behind. McDavid slowed his pace just enough to let the defenders cross in front of him. Meanwhile, he held on to the puck and gave them all the slip.

Suddenly there was no one left to beat but the goaltender. McDavid pulled the puck to his backhand. The goalie went down to make the stop, but McDavid pulled the puck back to his forehand. Then he flipped the puck into the net. Oilers fans jumped to their feet as the horn blasted. There was no doubt about it. McDavid was back.

ROOKIE AWARDS

Because of his collarbone injury, McDavid played just three full months during his rookie season. All three months he was named NHL Rookie of the Month. And despite missing so much time, McDavid was still a finalist for the Calder Memorial Trophy. That award is given to the NHL Rookie of the Year.

CCM
C
OILERS
CCM
OILERS

4 MOST VALUABLE PLAYER

Even though Connor McDavid missed half of his rookie year, he had a great season. With that in mind, fans wondered what he could do if he stayed healthy all year. They were about to find out.

The Oilers won seven of their first eight games of 2016–17. By the end of February, McDavid was leading the league in scoring. Everyone in Edmonton was thinking about the playoffs.

As the regular season wound down, the Oilers were on a roll. So was McDavid.

McDavid battles for the puck during a 2017 game against the San Jose Sharks.

Going into the last game, he needed just two more points to reach 100 for the season. An Oilers player hadn't done that in more than 20 years.

The final game of the season pitted Edmonton against the Vancouver Canucks. In the second period, McDavid got an assist on a goal by Drake Caggiula. That meant McDavid was just one point away from 100. But time was winding down.

Early in the third period, McDavid carried the puck down the right side, watching his two teammates coming with him. McDavid turned and passed the puck across the ice to Leon Draisaitl on the left. Draisaitl blasted it into the net. McDavid's assist gave him 100 points on the season. The Edmonton crowd started to chant, "MVP! MVP! MVP!"

Edmonton fans show their appreciation after McDavid scored his 100th point of the season.

McDavid and the Oilers made the playoffs for the first time in more than a decade. In the first round, they faced the defending Western Conference Champion San Jose Sharks. McDavid scored two goals in the series, helping his team win in six games.

The second round didn't end so well. The Oilers lost to the Anaheim Ducks in seven games. Still, McDavid's first full season was a big one. He won the scoring trophy and was voted league MVP both by the media and the players.

The 2017–18 season was harder on the Oilers. With 108 points, McDavid was the NHL's top scorer for the second year in a row. But it wasn't enough to send the Oilers back to the playoffs. There would be no chance at the Stanley Cup that season.

Unfortunately, 2018–19 was practically a repeat of the season before. McDavid was brilliant as usual, scoring 100 points for the third time in his career. But

TEAM LEADER

McDavid's second season in the NHL started off with a special honor. When a team picks a captain for the year, it's usually a veteran player who has experience in the league. McDavid was only 19 years old when the Oilers picked him to be their captain. He became the youngest captain in NHL history.

McDavid lights the lamp during a 2019 shootout against the Florida Panthers.

Edmonton missed the playoffs for the second season in a row. Even so, Oilers fans had hope for the future. With Connor McDavid on the team, another trip to the playoffs seemed like a good bet.

TIMELINE

1. **Richmond Hill, Ontario (January 13, 1997)**
   Connor McDavid is born in Richmond Hill, a town north of Toronto.

2. **Erie, Pennsylvania (April 7, 2012)**
   At the age of 15, Connor is drafted by the Erie Otters.

3. **Sunrise, Florida (June 26, 2015)**
   The Edmonton Oilers select McDavid as the first overall pick in the 2015 NHL Entry Draft.

4. **St. Louis, Missouri (October 8, 2015)**
   McDavid makes his NHL debut in a 3–1 loss to the St. Louis Blues.

5. **Dallas, Texas (October 13, 2015)**
   In a game against the Dallas Stars, McDavid scores his first NHL goal.

6. **Edmonton, Alberta (October 15, 2015)**
   The Edmonton Oilers hold their season home opener, giving fans their first look at the new star player on home ice.

7. **San Jose, California (April 12, 2017)**
   McDavid plays in his first NHL playoff game. The Oilers defeat the Sharks in the first round.

MAP

AT-A-GLANCE

Birth date: January 13, 1997

Birthplace: Richmond Hill, Ontario

Position: Center

Shoots: Left

Size: 6 feet 1 inch, 193 pounds

NHL team: Edmonton Oilers (2015–)

Previous team: Erie Otters (2012–2015)

Major awards: Art Ross Trophy (2016–17, 2017–18), Ted Lindsay Award (2016–17, 2017–18), Hart Memorial Trophy (2016–17)

Accurate through the 2018–19 season.

GLOSSARY

assist
A pass that results in a goal.

backhand
The outside of the stick blade.

breakaway
When a player has a clear path to the net with no defenders between him and the goalie.

captain
A team's leader.

crease
The area directly in front of the goalie, painted in blue.

draft
An event that allows teams to choose new players coming into the league.

forehand
The inside of the stick blade.

hat trick
A game in which a player scores three or more goals.

MVP
Most valuable player.

point
A statistic that a player earns by scoring a goal or having an assist.

sportsmanship
The act of treating opponents with respect and playing by the rules.

TO LEARN MORE

Books

Bates, Greg. *Connor McDavid: Hockey Star*. Lake Elmo, MN: Focus Readers, 2019.

Peters, Chris. *Hockey Season Ticket: The Ultimate Fan Guide*. Mendota Heights, MN: Press Box Books, 2019.

Peters, Chris. *Hockey's New Wave: The Young Superstars Taking Over the Game*. Mendota Heights, MN: Press Box Books, 2019.

Websites

Edmonton Oilers Official Site
https://www.nhl.com/oilers

Erie Otters Official Site
http://ottershockey.com

Team Canada Official Site
https://www.hockeycanada.ca/en-ca/team-canada

INDEX